THE DEVIL'S TOUR

D0838818

MARY KARR

THE DEVIL'S TOUR

A NEW DIRECTIONS BOOK

ACKNOWLEDGMENTS
Special thanks to the Mrs. Giles Whiting Foundation for a Writer's Award in
1989–90, to the Mary Ingraham Bunting Foundation at Radcliffe College for
a Fellowship in 1990–91, and to Michael Milburn for editing both patient and
ruthless.

Some of the poems in this book first appeared in the following magazines: *Co-
lumbia, The Harvard Review, The Harvard Gazette, Indiana Review, Parnassus,
Ploughshares, Poetry, The Radcliffe Quarterly, 3, TriQuarterly, Willow Springs.*

"Etching of the Plague Years" and "The Toddler as Cathedral" appeared in
Q&A: Interviews with Harvard Scholars (Harvard University Press, 1991), ed-
ited by Peter Costa; "Soft Mask" was anthologized in *Sutured Words: Poems
about Medicine* (Aviva Press, 1987), edited by John Mukand; "Post-Larkin
Triste" was reprinted in *Pushcart Prize XV* (Pushcart Press, 1990), edited by
Bill Henderson.

The epigraph on p. ix, from Allen Grossman's "The Piano Player Explains
Himself" (Copyright © 1988 by Allen Grossman), from *The Ether Dome and
Other Poems,* is reprinted by permission of New Directions Publishing Corpo-
ration.

Manufactured in the United States of America
New Directions Books are published on acid-free paper.
First published as New Directions Paperbook 768 in 1993
Published simultaneously in Canada by Penguin Books Canada Limited

Library of Congress Cataloging in Publication Data

Karr, Mary.
    The devil's tour / by Mary Karr.
       p. cm. — (New Directions paperbook ; 768)
    ISBN 0–8112–1231–9
    I. Title.
PS3561.A6929D4   1993
811'.54—dc20   92–42955
                                    CIP

New Directions books are published for James Laughlin
by New Direction Publishing Corporation,
80 Eighth Avenue, New York 10011

THIRD PRINTING

for Dev, born 1986
and for Stephen Dobyns
and Deborah Greenwald

Contents

. . . Behold,
I send the demon I know to relieve your need,
An imperfect player at the perfect instrument
Who takes in hand The Regulator of the World
To keep the splendor from destroying us.

Allen Grossman,
"The Piano Player Explains Himself"

COLEMAN

To while away the mosquito-humming night,
we crawled beneath the oil field fence,
and you straddled the pump as it bucked

a slow-motion rodeo. Fifteen and drunk
on apple wine, hiding in your Afro's shadow,
you wore the bruised imprint

of your father's palm with quiet chivalry.
I loved you inconsolably, though we never
touched: a boy from the docks, a cracker girl

preoccupied with books. We sealed ourselves
behind your van's curved windshield
like figures in a paperweight, played chess

by the dashboard's eerie light, dawn breaking
in chemical-pink sky, refinery towers looming
like giants from a fairy tale.

Once a swarm of boys we'd swapped insults with
since nursery school reared into view,
flung bricks and bottles we hotrodded

just beyond—my hair streaming
against the glass, your *a capella* song.
And in the book the vigilantes keep

in some back room of some bait shop,
they marked you from then on,
beat knots across your skull,

until your sawtooth smile said you knew
a spray of buckshot already loosed
was flying towards your eyes like stars in negative.

You made the papers as a hunting accident.
And your mom, answering the torn screen door
in the palest flowered dress, claimed God

had shaped you for an early grave.
When I finally caught a Greyhound north,
I wanted only to escape

the brutal limits of that town,
its square chained yards, pumps
that bowed so mindlessly to earth,

the raging pistons of that falling
dynasty. Coleman, you rode that ghost horse
hard and recklessly against the dark,

but could not break it. White pawn
to black knight, I travel always
towards your missing face.

DON GIOVANNI'S CONFESSOR

The Don withheld nothing, so at first
the old priest feared for his own virtue,
which had never been tested

by the powdered flanks of a duchess,
but hearing the litanized names,
the priest soon learned what all whores

know: it was never a pleasure.
That ceased right away. Even the tenderest
stalk of flesh grows calloused with work.

(Which only improves its performance.)
Rather the young man worshiped the instant
his pleas took hold, when a draped taffeta skirt

turned from window or looking glass
or any world but that which shone
on the orb of his eye, and she was silk

to his stone, heat to his cold.
It made him a god, that surrender.
The lies never mattered, nor did one

lady stand apart from the rest
prompting regret. Nothing so paltry
could touch him. Yet he was doomed

to loathe what he needed most, torso
after headless torso like serpents,
so lately even if sunk

in a perfumed bath, he felt his own skin
too tight round his being. And still desire
filled him and filled him with venom.

For the priest too, the stories got boring,
so much the same thing. Behind the screen
he lowered his face to the cage

of his hands, cocked his ear
beyond the locked cubicle—the line
of peasants shifting their burdens,

and outside, the Don's own horses jerked
at apple boughs with a whoosh of wet leaves
and jangled harness. The fruit thudded heavy

as bodies the priest long ago heard fall
where a great battle raged
and himself a boy crouched in a tree hull

among cobwebs and beetle husks. How at dusk
peering out, he saw the slack entrails of men
and their beasts entwine royal blue

and worm white and not
unlovely, and not unlike the clouds
God had sent down a fallen sword's length

to mark time till the mother arrived.
She lifted him as he'd been lifted
from darkness at birth: sun blind,

her loose woven shawl over his eyes
like a black grid through which the Don
now spoke to wake him, voice raspy

as flies' wings, and carnage
was once again carnage,
and he could think of no fair penance.

THE WORM-FARMER'S LAMENT

If you git work, write,
That's what they shouted after your great
and not-so great whomevers,
who trudged away down wagon ruts walking
so as not to piss off the mule, away
from Bumfuck, Georgia, Flathead, Tennessee,
the iron skillets strapped to their backs
receding into dots on the map,
while those remaining took up
pickaxes or lit candles
over their foreheads then descended
to various infernos.
                              The travelers had it no better:
bandits slit their throats; their oxen
fell sick and slobbered; their babies' faces
were masked in lengths of calico
they'd scrimped to buy.

And still, they bore it,
being washed forward like so much
gorgeous debris, ferried by will
and the dumb hope that by grunting up
the next hill, one could reach a clearing
gold with sunflowers and there
burdens could be unstrapped, boots
unlaced, and everyone could sink
knee-deep in a humming splendor.

That's wrong, of course.
History proves it.
Once you reach the final point
of all those roads cut by granite-faced
ancestors and even your own
forgettable efforts, then the spirit
is so stalled by arrival

that the long grasses become a cage,
the long fields blank

linoleum in a gleaming kitchen,
where you wonder how the chairs stand
so empty, and on certain nights,
with your full belly leaned into the sink
and cool water piped over your wrist,
you suddenly long to shove your arm
down the disposal or rest your head
in the trash compactor or just climb
in your not-quite-paid-for wagon
to breathe clouds till you can stop
breathing, stop sitting there and start

worm-farming, that thankless trade
no one wrote back about,
the quiet work for which you were born.

ALL THIS AND MORE

The Devil's tour of hell did not include
a factory line where molten lead
spilled into mouths held wide,

no electric drill spiraling screws
into hands and feet, nor giant pliers
to lower you into simmering vats.

Instead, a circle of light
opened on your stuffed armchair,
whose chintz orchids did not boil and change,

and the Devil adjusted
your new spiked antennae
almost delicately, with claws curled

and lacquered black, before he spread
his leather wings to leap
into the acid-green sky.

So your head became a tv hull,
a gargoyle mirror. Your doppelganger
sloppy at the mouth

and swollen at the joints
enacted your days in sinuous
slow motion, your lines delivered

with a mocking sneer. Sometimes
the frame froze, reversed, began
again: the red eyes of a friend

you cursed, your girl child cowered
behind the drapes, parents alive again
and puzzled by this new form. That's why

you clawed your way back to this life.

POST-LARKIN TRISTE

The day you died a cold New England wind
stung the air I breathed, and on the street
faces erased themselves as I approached.
For several blocks, I shadowed a big

round-shouldered man built like a pear,
plaid scarf and tweedy overcoat.
Sir, I almost said a hundred times,
but he escaped as you escaped,

my one careful fan letter returned
unopened; the night I'd hitched
the length of England under thunderheads
your window glowed pure rose.

There you stood wiping off a plate,
the last romantic, a sliver of fire
flickered in your eye. I didn't knock
or climb the stair. When you carried

your milk bottle to the stoop,
you briefly stared my way as if you knew
I crouched there in the garden mud,
my vision blurry with the sleet.

Then stepping through the door,
you sank from view, and later from our lives.
What might I have said to you?
That you were loved perhaps, that love's

a cure. I wanted to hold your large
white hands in mine and say
I understood until you yielded
all your pent-up hurt and wept

as you once said you did alone
safe in the bubble of your car
hearing Wordsworth read on the radio.
Instead I watched you glower at the night.

The cloudy, dread-locked moon reflected
in your spectacles was a face
I didn't dare to meet of someone
swooping towards us with a message, then away.

ROUNDS

In the night nurse's hand, the flashlight
sends a dime-sized beam, so the new girl, unused
to suicide patrols, starts up and briefly sees

a phantom holding fire. Then dark returns.
The girl studies the spackled ceiling
where the smoke alarm blinks like a satellite

launched to track her movements or lack
thereof, for she has stalled in herself,
lonely and visited by the old wishes.

She wants the moon, for instance, now sliced
by long bars into three neat pieces to become
the eye of God she watched for on summer nights lying

in a meadow swaying with clover, the earth
curved gently against her back as Sputnik
spidered across Orion. Later she'd eat a dish

of ice cream at the sink, still later wait
for her door to open and a triangle of light
to spill her parents' shadows forward—

her mom large-breasted, her dad deceptively
square in cotton boxers. She still felt safe
when he watched her resting. The nubbly code

of the bedspread was still meaningless.
But his shadow turned to lead, once her own breasts
started like soft stones and she sought messages

where none were written. The phantom lover,
longed for, failed to appear,
so had to be shaped from inner phosphorus

and sleep and air. Then her hands were busy
on herself, and her father's care
fell across her, a cold iron. His shadow

blackened everything, while he himself
vanished. She lay unillumined then,
but for the green angel distantly glowing

on the light switch, and whatever stabbed in
from sky or street. *Whaddya want,
the moon?* he asked as he stroked

her pale geography, as if it ended there,
and no nurse would come at painful intervals
to shoot that beam at her blank third eye.

LUNCH

for Michael

In the hours since breakfast I traveled the world's
obstacle course to reach you—rode my slot
in traffic, scaled countless hills of paper
as voices wormed through phone cords to my ear
where I kept your moist words from the night before
boxed all morning.
              This afternoon
I wait for you in our favorite fishhouse.
The trees need darning, the autumn sky
is the pale gray of an oyster,
and the second you lumber into view—
your arms loaded with books, your angular
patrician face calmly bewildered—
the old thunder starts in my chest, my every road
has led me here to you: checkered cloth, garlic
squid, the familiar tongue forever strange.

ETCHING OF THE PLAGUE YEARS

In the valley of your art history book,
the corpses stack in the back of a cart
drawn by an ox whose rolling shoulder muscles
show its considerable weight.

He does this often. His velvet nostrils
flare to indicate the stench.

It's the smell you catch after class
while descending a urine-soaked
subway stair on a summer night
in a neighborhood where cabs won't drive:
the odor of dead flowers, fear
multiplied a thousand times.

The train door's hiss
seals you inside with a frail boy
swaying from a silver hoop.
He coughs in your direction, his eyes
are burn holes in his face.

Back in the fourteenth-century print
lying in your lap, a hand
white as an orchid has sprouted
from the pyramid of flesh.
It claws the smoky air.

Were it not for that,
the cart might carry green cordwood
(the human body knobby and unplaned).

Wrap your fingers around your neck
and feel the stony glands.
Count the holes in your belt loop

for lost weight.
In the black unfurling glass,
study the hard planes of your face.

Compare it to the prom picture
in your wallet, the orchid
pinned to your chest like a spider.

Think of the flames
at your high school bonfire
licking the black sky, ashes rising,
innumerable stars. The fingers that wove
with your fingers
have somehow turned to bone.

The subway shudders between dark and light.
The ox plods across the page.

Think of everyone
you ever loved: the boy
who gets off at your stop
is a faint ideogram for each.

Offer him your hand.
Help him climb the stair.

AVERAGE TORTURE

It's not the child's nightmare slide
down a ten-foot razor into a bath
of alcohol, nor the cobra's hooded stare
suddenly come near, but the multiplying string
of insignificance that's become your life.

The doorbell chimes, a phone
jars you from your book.
Your balding pharmacist recounts
the longest dullest joke
in history, his jaw hinged
like a puppet's *blah*
and blah and blah as you stitch
a smile across your face. A cop
drags you from your slot
in traffic: go straight to court, wait
for hours, weep shamelessly
to save ten bucks.

Such aggressively minor suffering
wins no handshakes, roses, accolades
and threatens to suck the soul out,

though in a small compartment in your skull
you hope for finer things.
At night you set aside your lists
and dime-sized aches to lift its lid
and find the simple room
in which everything you meant to speak
and shape and do is spoken,
formed and done: thirty-odd
thousand jasmine-scented nights
opening like satin umbrellas
all at once. But less and less

you unlatch paradise.
You learn to sleep through days, standing
like a beast, sleep while turning pages
or crying out from love. You sleep
and sleep. One day you wake up dead.
Strange hands raise you from your bed.
The zipper's jagged teeth interlock
before your shining eyes. Small world.

GETTING READY FOR THE GARBAGE MAN

All alleys end here tonight,
your plastic bags obese
with carcasses and coffee grounds,

all Sunday's helpings gone rot.
You clatter softly. A fine sleet
pellets your hide slippers.

Your face steams gray in the vapors.
Looking up into the bowl of night,
you miss the intricate machine

Galileo sketched: his planets
sturdy bearings in their chutes;
yours only lurch. The shining cars

sleep in dank garages. Children sleep
hugging terrified bears.
Only your mind rambles loose in its chamber,

which lacks any splendor.
Even the squat garbage cans glimmer
more than you, armored sentries,

dumb and waiting for dawn as ordered.

DISAPPOINTMENTS OF THE APOCALYPSE

Once warring factions agreed upon the date
and final form the apocalypse would take,
and whether dogs and cats and certain trees
deserved to sail, and if the dead would come or be left
a forwarding address, then opposing soldiers
met on ravaged plains to shake hands
and postulate the exact shade
of the astral self—some said lavender,
others gray. And physicists rocketed
copies of the decree to paradise
in case God had anything to say,
the silence that followed being taken
for consent, and so citizens
readied for celestial ascent.

Those who hated the idea stayed indoors
till the appointed day. When the moon
clicked over the sun like a black lens
over a white eye, they stepped out
onto porches and balconies to see
the human shapes twist and rise
through violet sky and hear trees uproot
with a sound like enormous zippers
unfastening. And when the last grassblades
filled the air, the lonely vigilants fell
in empty fields to press their bodies
hard into dirt, hugging their own outlines.

Then the creator peered down from his perch,
as the wind of departing souls tore the hair
of those remaining into wild coronas,
and he mourned for them as a father
for defiant children, and he knew that each
small skull held, if not some vision

of his garden, then its aroma of basil
and tangerine washed over by the rotting sea.
They alone sensed what he'd wanted
as he first stuck his shovel into clay
and flung the planets over his shoulder,
or used his thumbnail to cut smiles and frowns
on the first blank faces. Even as the saints
arrived to line before his throne singing
and a wisteria poked its lank blossoms
through the cloudbank at his feet,
he trained his gaze on the deflating globe
where the last spreadeagled Xs clung like insects,
then vanished in puffs of luminous smoke,

which traveled a long way to sting his nostrils,
the journey lasting more than ten lifetimes.
A mauve vine corkscrewed up from the deep
oblivion, carrying the singed fume
of things beautiful, noble, and wrong.

DONNA GIOVANNA'S FAILURE

When he left there was nothing
she could keep. She'd sold the golden
chains, the emerald and intaglio

in temper fits. The silks
she'd burnt with the scented notes.
The birds were freed.

The mare was put to sleep.
The stable man had long since crushed
the cameo portrait to dust.

So from their decade of pleasure
nothing. Even memory refused
to hold him, for in his quest

for novelty and from fear
of being perceived as dull,
he had defied all habit.

He could enter and kneel
like a priest or greet her
with a glove slap. Yet once

the earth split and he fell
to the burning lake,
his absence brought her no peace.

The men she took in his place
were grateful at first, but soon sensed
her petulance with their techniques.

She too quickly sighed, too quickly
turned away. Mornings, she gazed
flatly at a certain chair as though

some phantom sat witness there.
The other men were mere stick figures.
They came to see themselves that way

till she summoned no one.
Then the priest's coach rolled fast
over the black fields

for he hoped that she'd repent.
But she claimed all she knew
of grace she'd learned in sin.

She threw out the mirrors,
the paintings and books. Beauty
was painful. Alone in her firelit

chamber, she wondered if her great love
rose from the sparks what shape
he might assume, and if he'd ride

some female demon in whalebone corset
writhing for his touch into the room.
Would he draw back the quilt,

burrow beneath her eyelet gown
to breathe her salt air
in weak thirst? Or plunge

hard up her rump without ambergris?
Handle her like glass or like
a farm beast? Which touch was his?

Which could she fairly miss and which
begrudge as false? Years passed.
She lay untouched and wet to her core.

And who then burned in the hotter hell?

THE UNWEEPABLES

See them rise from the coiling waves,
history's lost women, unbowing their heads
and lifting frail shoulders
against the bruised night sky.

A storm is coming, but the moon persists.
And in my solar plexus and below
where I cleave against myself into the birth
chamber, I recognize our likeness,

these ghosts the color of lit celery
(o bright) and unscriptured, forgotten even
by their children's children
whom they suckled inadvertently

and who warmed them not at all. More than a few
are limbless, and all are wounded by neglect—
smashed noses, sliced breasts, and beneath
the black mirrored sea, in the cerulean

fathoms from which they rose, the amber silt
shifts from their rising like the frieze
of a great battle erasing itself in a sandstorm.
Theirs is a silent parade, advancing in place.

The moon above them is a sour aspirin
unmarked, for women leave no wake
with their long thighs, no thread
or twisting umbilicus, though their tears

could overflow this ocean, drown us all.

SMALL BUT URGENT REQUEST
TO THE UNKNOWABLE

for Thomas Lux

Whatever small nugget of kindness we carry,
that shy opal I picture buried deep in gray folds
of a cortex evolved to flinch at fire
and whittle sharp sticks when beasts
stalk to close; whatever prompts

bereaved widows to offer you coffee then
the guestbook, and parched sailors adrift
to share the day's thimble of water,
and mothers to lift the most bent and broken
children with joy and glad for the work of it;

whatever iota of caring has survived
the millennia's hardships, ice age and terror
and the simple tedium of walking upright—
maybe it's no bigger now than a seed
in a fig—tonight I call for it, call

with my dry mouth from this cold room
clouded by my being alive
on a planet whose true gravity
eludes me; let that pinprick of light
multiply in the sky's nightly leather

and in the pupil of each eye. Let me seek it
in the large, crazed creatures whose shadows
I fear most, in myself, for instance.
Kneeling, I poke at this ash-heaped hearth in hope
of some faint imagining, grateful for that.

MEMOIRS OF A CHILD EVANGELIST

Long before your bronze head topped the pulpit,
you spoke in tongues, and the dirt-streaked faces
peered up blank and white as dinner plates
from folding chairs in steamy circus tents.

After Bible study, you explored
the catacombs of your mother's hair,
which you unwove from its wobbly tower
and brushed so blue sparks filled the room.

You burned but were not consumed, and when alone
a demon rose between your legs and stared
with its slitted eye: another sign
of goodness, to be tempted, tested.

You shall take up serpents, the Bible says,
so you lifted cottonmouths from a wooden box,
drank strychnine under plywood crosses,
and town after town appeared

in your bug-flecked windshield.
Dunking one white-robed girl at dawn,
you washed her sins away, and later
forced yourself into her quietest place.

The church van rocked and rocked,
and she was silenced by your prayer cloth
strapped across her open mouth, a bloody snake
winding down her leg. Suddenly you knew

each body was a room with something
evil locked inside. You thought of aging
women, of men so sad and sick they'd press
their hands against t.v. screens

for your warmth. On the camera's
unremitting glass you watch your tongue
writhing like a slug. You talk and talk.
The human ear is a well,

the skull a cavern lit by nothing
but *I want, I want,* till the director
rakes a hand across his throat, and the lights
dim slowly as extinguished suns.

SAD RITE

Because I was empty
my body got me a child,
the small idea of a child—
some pearly cells and light.
I thought of it all night.
It still lacked hands
or a face with which to fill
its hands, or another, lovelier
face to fill its heart.
Because I tend
to take myself apart, I planned
to scoop it out, this child, but keep
the idea, being cursed
with keeping and ideas,
with emptiness. And so I did.
And so I keep
a small abyss inside
until the moon is right.
And then I find a bar, a man
who'll neatly stack my empties
while he drags his sour cloth
across my place, and I read omens
in the clouds he makes, until the moon
comes down when I rise up, its red light
a blade; inside me bloody flame.

ACCUSING MESSAGE FROM DEAD FATHER

In the dream you phone
from the kingdom of the dead
to absolve me. No one shoved
your long corpse into the crematorium,
just a man-sized log of creosote,
a morbid joke.
The black-mouthed stove's hissing sparks
echo our poor connection.
Last we spoke ten years ago
my betrayal was in progress:
the attendants slid you into the ambulance
while Mother hid sobbing in the garage,
and the sunburnt driver promised
to ferry you to the home I'd chosen—
the one least infernal, least
urinous, with the least surly nurses.
Your penis lay slack along your leg
and I carried the warm bottle
of piss with the dignity you used
to keep thugs at bay in bars
where you cautioned me to step
straight, not speak, avoid all eyes
till we're safe in the truck—
and even my betrayal you bore
stoically till our gazes locked
in that white tin box,
and you cried the last hard word
unscooped from your skull—*bad*
and *bad* and *bad* . . .
In the dream I say *Mea
culpa,* and you say don't
matter much no more,
and upon waking, I find
in the phone machine's black window

a red *one* glowing
like a limbless man,
who plays back as a click,
dial tone careening into quiet.

THE LEGION

That they should never leave
the Lone Star State had been
the fondest wish of each
so when each floated back
or scraped down from Seoul
or Auschwitz or Saigon,
he took a seat at this
besparkled bar, where the line
of wobbly heads glides a greeting
then retreats, bows
to the ounce-high shot
of liquid in each fist.
Gulp and guzzle: emptiness;
lifted finger: more. Repeat
repeat. And in the mirror
behind a pyramid of bottles
shine separate pairs of glassy eyes
that have ceased to note tattoos
of serpents coiling up thick arms
and women's names embroidered
in the skin of wrists.
I never enter but I wince
at all the pain that goes ignored,
and at the place my father kept—
an ox-blood colored stool
that skewered him to earth
those last few years now sits
like the last dot in an ellipsis
heading to oblivion. He orphaned me
by accident. He wandered
fearful in his skull (the human mind can hold
so much) stranded before shallow bowls
of cheddar goldfish, jars of bulging
pickled eggs and pigs' feet

you have to suck to gristle
for the sour meat.
Above the formica bar's
scattered constellations
he must have reached (please god)
that endless Lone Star State again,
his comrades aging boys
wearing dusty overalls, jungle camouflage,
pale fatigues stick-figured into men.

DAY-CARE FIELD TRIP: AQUARIUM

for David Foster Wallace

The squid pumps past trailing pale tentacles.
Then the ray like a poisonous angel
lists and tilts away
to reveal beneath its furled wing
a pie-dough face, befuddled
as mine in the aquarium glass, against which
my hand splays to stroke the luminous eel
or to pop the bubbles that whorl
from the diver's mask.

He dispenses lettuce from his sack
most gently. His tanks and awkwardness
prove there are other worlds.
And the way the shark's muscular S
bulges toward me then contracts
away like a swinging bludgeon proves
that sight can lie, space
can lie as we guess it.

I could gape all day at that in disbelief,
and at the underwater thumps that stir
the fathomless bones in my ear,
all the meaningless pulses
of sensation I can't grasp because
they are nameless and no spot
in my skull can hold them.
I would suck myself to this cool wall
as the octopus seeks whatever
doesn't move. Instead
                    I move,
climb the spiral ramp around the tank
bumped by lines of schoolkids
clung to ropes by which their teachers
trail them to the top—a sky of scum

and one-celled stars, long mosses
willowing, lung-filling silence and rot.
When the gnarled head of the turtle breaks
the surface, he draws a gasp.
So the o-shaped mouths briefly frost
the foot-deep glass. What a class

portrait that would make: the row
of faces, each breathing a foggy zero
like the clouds of good advice our ancestors
peering down must long to speak—*Take care*
of all your teeth. Get sleep. Be
true. Watch out. We must look so dumb and bright
to them, our eyes brimming with monsters and gods.

SOFT MASK

On the ultrasound screen my child curled
in his own fluid orbit, less real
than any high-school textbook tadpole
used to symbolize birth, till the nurse
placed a white arrow on his heart flicker:
a quick needle of light. Tonight his face

blooms in my window before trees
stripped bare, a moon hung full and red.
That soft mask, not yet hardened in autumn wind,
would hold a thumbprint if I touched him. I hesitate
to touch him. He's not yet felt the burden
of a hand, nor tasted air, nor wobbled
toward some bladelike gaze, his mouth
smudged against the clear silk
that envelops him, webbed hands that reach
and retreat as a cat tests water.

Or like Narcissus, or the great wondering
madonnas, or any beast lost in another, the demon
who kneels to feed at some lily throat:
his pulse first matching then at odds with mine,
that small arrow seeming to tremble
as if striking something true.

THE DRIVEN

for Lecia

It is always raining when you meet, and dark.
At night's end, one always drives the other
to his or her respective car,
for you like to meet nowhere,
across no table, no swan-necked orchid
between you. Between you,
there is only this silence
unbridgeable. You do not touch,
so there is none of the confusion
of touching. The wipers seem to sweep and smear
the shining road. Where are you traveling
in such awful weather? The question remains
unspoken, for yours is a drama of nuance.
A sharp intake of breath indicates pain,
a slant stare bewilderment,
and the eighty-seven brands
of silence you exchange merely vary
the theme of loss. And the one who leaves
without umbrella always feels the other's
headlights snail across the back—o lost glance
and lost caress—and stands an instant
in the downpour breathless.

IN ILLO TEMPORE

for Tom Johnson (1950–86)

You curl like a creature in a shell,
scooped of words, but still humming
the Schubert you drilled into those
you tutored. Our fingers in rubber gloves
interlock with yours as we arch
over you in a strange heart shape,
watch the orange juice you sip
climb the straw's spiral,
the way mercury rises to red notches
to mark the fever they can't stop.

The cherub-faced intern points
to his clipboard and shakes his blond curls
while Easter bells resound
among the book stalls and college bars
where we were young.

Later, we peel off our paper gowns and masks,
oil your dry hands with ours, comb
your falling hair, and Michael leans
his ear to your cracked mouth to name
each rest and black key in your song.
It is a form of talk, this naming, long
rehearsed, unlike the later silence.

WINTER IN THE CITY OF FRIENDSHIP

Friend, some nights when I smoke on the fire escape,
I search beyond the snow-plowed streets
to the cold blue light of the study
in the tower in which you've walled yourself,
surrounded by minions and the books
that bolster your arguments.

Who will question you in this place?
You exile those who question, and your eyes,
which sometimes wheel this way
like searchlights do not make me out,
but cast the bright interior
shape of your face across mine.
Over and over, you erase me this way.

Still, I know the last kind word
that passed between us must circle
your tower. A small white bird,
it pecks your sill, songless,
its heart thrumming dimly.
It will not leave you,
however heavy the shade you draw,
however broad the back you turn.
It taps the frosted glass with a sound
like tiny iron letters embossed
against parchment, keys pressed
by fingers on a hand you refuse
to reach for, however much alone.

ERECTUS

for Walt Mink

First the claws withdrew, and the tusks receded;
at the tip of each digit a sheer window
of hammered bone, and only one serious

triangle of hair remained on each adult body.
The tough hides softened so we appeared
edible to one another. Teeth

hid in our mouths, and in the long hollows
of our limbs long bones hid
to remind us of the old armors.

And now crowning the spine's knotty stalk,
the skull shields a pearl-gray brain.
Though all the hard parts of ourselves

retreated there, it bears no orbit
of thorns, and sliced with a scalpel shows only
more of itself. You can hold it in one hand

or cup it in two to show reverence.
Hurl it as you may hard
against a wall, it cannot weep,

for it is eyeless, yet secretly believes
you could die and it could go on
living without you. Sad

to think of all that impotent will
sealed in a bowl where no light shines,
and the only breezes imagined.

A limbless wizard thus encaged,
it has no hand to wave a hazel branch,
nor tongue to unleash the old spells,

but anyway it could not know those gods
died long ago. But first were planted in our heads
these brains, these wrinkled bulbs

that read down the spines' long roots.
Yet all we know leads to a sharp cliff face,
a repetitive gray sea tugged

into countless dunce caps,
above which we stand in thirsty awe.
We should bury our dead

atop the earth, skulls tilted back
that blind stars might peer down
at our bones akimbo

and observe our giving way to rock,
rock to fossil, eyeholes
filled with sand, flooded with dawn.

BAYOU

for Pete Karr

I heap your corpse with flowers
then commend it to the flames, stumble
from the funeral home to row this wobbly boat
across the bayou that you loved.

My arms ache. The sun is high and white,
and you appear in vines that trail my shoulder
like your hand, the cyprus a gnarled man,
amber locust husks scooped clean of flesh

your flesh. And when the alligator drops
his second eyelid like a veil, I wonder
if you keep some pearly watch through cloud
or mist. Bullfrogs drone my answer, death

and death again. Without your balance or grace,
I somehow reach the reeds, bait my hook
and cast, feel your strength in the sudden
tug, the shining line like a cord

strung through me, plucked and singing.

HER ONE BAD EYE

for my mother

The mist crept over the iris
like spider's silk, then the doctor's
scalpel slipped, and everything went red

inside her head.
Then dark. She wore a black patch.
With her black umbrella

folded in on itself,
she dueled with my azaleas
to make light of her blindness.

My toddler son thought it funny
to lead her unexpectedly
off curbs or into low shrubs.

Off booze and pills at seventy,
with books her only opiates,
she had to hold large print

an inch behind the bulging
magnifier, and even then
she lost the thread of syntax.

She listened to jazz
through headphones waiting
all summer for the call.

Finally, an old man died.
His eyeballs were whisked
crosstown in a jar of milk, to Mass

Eye, then we arrived.
After the gauze was off,
she had a new blue eye

with a nick in it,
like a fault in ice.
I don't believe the body

stores events, so the eye
can't tell what it's seen anymore
than she can recount

to me her life's saga
in a way that makes sense.
We are dead to each other

that way, though she opened
her body to let me shine
weeping into this world,

and sometimes I feel her
looking through me to
that other world. Blind, this way

we stare at each other like corpses.

GRACE

for Marie

I have a friend whose mass
of hair electrifies the winter air,
weighs down her thin shadow
so she doesn't ascend, weaves
around her small face like intellect.
When I see her sail my way
in gray January, even if sorry
for myself and dead
to the regular beauties,
she lifts me with that wing
of honey light, one of the last
true wonders, who doesn't need
these words to mark
her grace, nor all that grace
herself. She gives it free.

CROUP

When he stands to cough the syrup from his lungs,
I arrive to sponge him cool, and he cries no
and no and no, the only syllable

to keep him whole. Today while staring through the O
in his last Cheerio, he mastered *all* and *gone*.
Then later came to fear his polar bear

would soon unravel in the wash, crib dismantle
where he stands, footsteps vanish where he walks,
for where he walks, I walk, and everywhere

my shadow falls. In bed, he cannot find
the shadow's edge, so stands and screams
in the crib's landing strip of starlight

like a small beast shaken from the moon.
I lift him, tote him to a stony room,
twist some knobs, rock him in warm steam.

Only in sickness will he rest
his cheek against my breast.
How heavy he feels in the vapors

refusing to merge into one creature.

PARENTS TAKING SHAPE

While his head wouldn't clear the chair seat,
the parents' voices traveled on a higher plane,
circled like wind, though his mom often stooped

down from her rainy mist of perfume
to lipstick a kiss upon his cheek, and his dad
hoisted him light as a ghost

to play airplane among the lamps,
which hung like so many dusty suns.
Eventually, he grew toward them,

and their fluid gibberish receded
into words, bounded by hard consonants
and fricatives. And their faces

once vague as clay hardened into masks
of monsters. They roamed paths amid
enormous furniture, hurling glass

objects whose exploding shards
prefigured for an instant in the air
the shapes of busted, starry gods.

Now he longs for the old ignorance, to squat again
in their treelike shadows fingering
the carpet's grass, or simply to feel for the end

of his own hand toward them. His mouth
thirsts for the word to change them
back. But he clings dumb to the table,

where their reflections hurl fast and random
as planets whirled from their axes, and the gravity
of each pulls a milky tide inside his head, side

to side, and how will he ever choose?

THE TODDLER AS CATHEDRAL

for Dev

He stands at the table longing
to take this ocean of wood
in his mouth where he can chew it whole.
He pounds and croons: table song, wood song,

song of rising on two legs
only, so the world shrinks from him.
How boldly he stands
in his solid cathedral of bone,

slapping his shadow, which spreads
large across the table's surface.
It's like a black man-sized suit
he will grow into, or like

the hole in the earth he'll someday
fill. Wavering on its edge, he seems
to know that, yet ignores the two figures
sunk in the sofa's flowers, how they call him

back from the shadow's abyss.
Instead, he retreats
to the sweet shape of his own mind,
that graceful canoe no one can touch,

and into which he might step.

MASS EYE AND EAR: THE WARD

My hand quivers as I light your cigarette.
The flame won't shrink your pupils,
stained tornado black and edged with cloud. Young,
I glimpsed the world inverted and swirling
on those eyes as you twirled on a barstool,
or drove blind drunk—the road's white dashes

sailing into them like knives.
This morning I poised a mascara wand
at your lashes' slope, and in a trick of light
your eye overlaid my eye. I blinked back
thirty years, saw seven golden circles
float in the hazel starburst there

like the seven wedding rings I found
tarnished in velvet boxes, sunk in rivers
of lingerie—seven men divorced, two kids
lost in a custody fight. The night you sketched
twin ladders at your wrists as if to climb
from your skin forever, their stares sent

India ink streaming down your cheek,
and attic rain erased the chalk portraits
you made and rolled into telescopes.
Only your face remains from the story,
as soft in my hands tonight as clay,
the banked cheekbones, the temples' shallows.

And I know every glint and fracture
of these eyes, which whiten now like breath
on a mirror as I lean close to fix your face.
I would paint them this way—
through your bridal veil of smoke, your milky gaze
fixed on my countenance vanishing.

FINAL POSITION

No pillow on earth could have kept
that crook from her neck,
which bends like a stalk, so each day
she must watch her calloused feet
curve into talons, and can't see
Death approach, just the shadow of him,
strangely reminiscent of her father
in his black rain slicker
on the night the horses escaped
and he slammed in and hit her for nothing,
and the big question mark
sprouted in her body cavity, drawing her
into this final position.

AGAINST NATURE

for Raymond Carver

I always loved the kick
of a shotgun jolting my arm socket
when squatting in waders before dawn
to pluck some mallard
from the sky's black arrowhead,
with dogs baying and loping through cattails.
Then later, walking home through swamp gas,
the greenheads a heavy
iridescent bouquet thumping my leg.

Thread a worm on a hook?
Gut a coon, sear a steak,
boil bristles from a hog?
Not chores I like, but tolerable.

*

God ordained that the rattler
who sleeps in the fallen pine
must sink its stone fangs
in the child's pale ankle,
just as the boy's heart must clench
at the first flush of venom—
the cold climbing his shins.
Then the snake decides this loud
thing is too big to eat
and slithers off, a mere ripple
in razor grass. And the boy's mother
must forever bear (even as worms
meander her ribcage) a leather pouch
on a thong drawn tight on a snippet
of hair. Yet the boy never flickers
through the minds of descendants, who lack

his name inscribed in the Bible
or mossy rock in a mudyard.

And at this and its variations
I lodge protest with whatever form
god assumes. Let god grow fat
on the fruit of this rotting garden.
Let him wear the necklace of bones
and dandle the beasts he's cast
like charms from any point on high
or down deep you care to believe.
Let him hallelujah the orgy of stars
in their hopeless intaglio.

Give me a book by a peasant, a poem
of thanks by a man whose lungs
fill with tumors. You should listen
for a month to Mozart writing
his own requiem—how many angels
crowded that small skull cavity,
the quill poised over an arctic
of parchment, the high voices fading.

*

The first sketches of a herd
fleeing a shower of arrows
must have been chalked by a woman
who'd felt a child writhe in her arms.

I light a torch to worship
her stonework, imagine her breast slack
and the child's limbs growing stiff.
Maybe she knelt to scoop earth
over his face before leaving
to follow the hoofprints. Maybe his
are the gnawed bones that rest
encased in glass.

I hope she beat that snake flat
with a rock before it escaped, charred
and devoured its meat, strapped
the new baby grazing her nipple
to her heartbeat with the patterned skin,
so the music of rattles lulled him.
The mounds of earth shrank
behind the tribe, what was murdered
carved on a cave wall, advancing forever.

DIVORCE

Boys from my class came to help
my husband lift the great antiques
his parents would inquire about:

cherry highboard, butler's table,
the four-poster bed on which
the Prime Minister once slept.

Without them, the house was cavernous.
I let our son skateboard in the dining room
where only my tag-sale buffet stood guard

over the impossibly long floorboards.
The blinds, raised, let in a world
of leafy dark. Past midnight

the cat, who'd navigated an exact number
of chair legs all his life,
couldn't find his bowl in all that

space. While I slept on my floor pallet,
he pounced and rabbit-kicked my head.
I had to disentangle from my hair

all four sets of claws, then tossed him
out into the pyramid of boxes
we'd erected in the yard.

Back on the futon, I could suddenly see
the VCR's digital clock blink off
and on like a tiny blank marquee.

In the middle of the night
there'd been a power failure.
It was zero o'clock, day zero.

I didn't know what could happen next.

Mary Karr received a 1990 appointment to the Bunting Institute at Radcliffe College and a 1989 Whiting Writers Award. Her individual poems won the Aarvon International Poetry Competition in 1987 and 1988, as well as *Poetry* magazine's Tietjens Award in 1990. She has also received grants from the National Endowment for the Arts and the Massachusetts Arts Council. Wesleyan published her first book, *Abacus,* in 1987. She has taught at Tufts, Harvard, and Sarah Lawrence. Her essays have appeared in *Poetry, American Poetry Review, Parnassus,* and *Pushcart XVII.* In 1995, Viking/Penguin published her memoir, *The Liars' Club,* which was a finalist for the National Book Critics Circle award and has since appeared on numerous bestseller lists across the country. She now teaches poetry in the graduate writing program at Syracuse University.